My First Book About

AIRPLANES and ROCKETS

By Kama Einhorn

Illustrated by Christopher Moroney

Random House 🏠 New York

Hello, everybodee! It is I, your furry blue friend Professor Grover. Today I am going to take you up, up, and away on an exciting journey. Right now, my friend Elmo has his head in the clouds. That is, he wants to know all about *airplanes* and *rockets*! Airplanes and rockets are machines that fly. Do you want to learn about them, too? Then please join us on our flight. If you are ready for takeoff, pretend to fasten your seat belt.

Airplanes & Rockets

People have always watched birds use their wings to fly.

Canada geese

Oh, hello there. Not all birds can fly, you know. I can't fly, but I do have lots of friends who can.

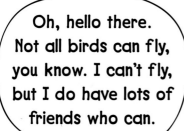

GROVER'S HOMEWORK

Go outside and look for some birds. Watch how their wings flap. What do you think it would be like to be a bird? Where would you go? What would you see?

A long time ago, people tried and tried to create machines that could fly.

After many, many years of trying and many experiments that didn't work, people finally invented airplanes—machines that could fly.

As little boys, brothers Orville and Wilbur Wright wondered how birds could fly. When they grew up, they built the very first airplane that actually flew!

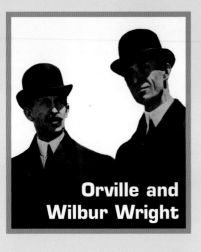

Orville and Wilbur Wright

the Wright brothers' first flight

Bye-bye, birdie!

airplane landing

Air is all around you. You cannot see it, but when it moves, you *can* see leaves blowing and kites flying.

In some ways, an airplane is similar to a car. They both have an engine and wheels that make them go.

As an airplane moves forward very fast on the ground, air underneath the wings pushes the whole airplane up off the ground. This is called **lift**.

When a plane leaves the ground, that is called **takeoff**. When it comes back down, that is called **landing**.

I have a little trouble with the takeoff part, but I'm really good at landing!

Today there are many different kinds of planes that can carry people and can travel very far, very fast.

Planes are made up of lots of different parts.

cabin door
cockpit
fuselage
wing
tail
nose
engines
wheels

Passengers are the people riding in a plane. **Cargo** is anything else that the plane may be carrying—suitcases, mail, or goods that are being delivered to another part of the world.

The **fuselage** holds the cabin, where the passengers sit and the cargo is stored.

The **pilot** and **co-pilot** fly the plane. They sit in the cockpit. In the cockpit are all the instruments the pilots use to fly the plane.

cockpit

This family is traveling someplace far from home. They can get there faster by flying than by driving. If you have ever been on an airplane, what do you remember about the flight?

Very large airplanes often fly above the clouds in the sky. Smaller planes, especially ones that carry only one or two people, fly much lower.

Did you know there is a machine that can go much, much higher and faster than an airplane? That machine is called a rocket. Turn the page to see what Earth looks like from a rocket ship in space!

A rocket is a very powerful engine that is used to power spacecraft.

Rockets help spacecraft **launch**, or shoot straight up from the ground, all the way into space. After a spacecraft gets far away from Earth, it can travel along on its own without the help of a rocket.

Gravity is an invisible force that pulls people and objects toward the ground on Earth. In space, there is no gravity, so astronauts and their spacecraft can float!

Earth as seen from space

When a rocket carries a spacecraft off the ground into space, that's called **liftoff**.

When a rocket carrying a spacecraft is about to take off into space, the scientists in charge of the rocket count down!

Wow, Elmo, you are a real rocket scientist! And I, Professor Grover, know that when a rocket returns from space to Earth's atmosphere, that is called **reentry**. The **atmosphere** is the air around Earth.

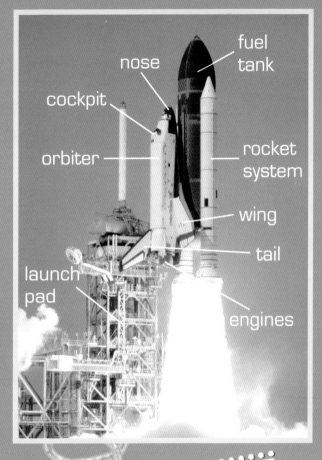

nose

cockpit

orbiter

fuel tank

rocket system

wing

tail

launch pad

engines

GROVER'S HOMEWORK

Count backward from ten to zero. When you get to zero, say, "Blastoff!" and jump into the air, pretending to be a rocket.

Astronauts are the pilots of spacecraft. They are the explorers of space.

Astronauts eat, sleep, and work in their spacecraft. They take pictures and do experiments that help them—and us—learn more about Earth, space, the sun, the moon, and other planets.

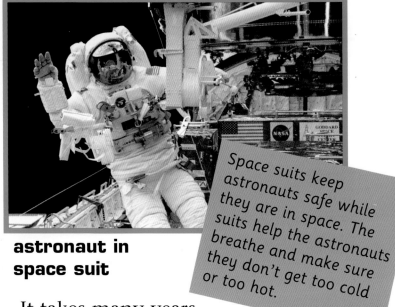

astronaut in space suit

Space suits keep astronauts safe while they are in space. The suits help the astronauts breathe and make sure they don't get too cold or too hot.

space

It takes many years of study and practice to become an astronaut.

This astronaut, Dr. Mae Jemison, is floating inside her spacecraft.

Whether they fly high or low, across the sky or straight up into the air, flying machines help people in many ways.

Crop dusters help farmers by dropping pesticides on many plants at once. This protects the plants from bugs and disease.

Rockets power spacecraft, which help us explore and learn about the world we live in and beyond.

Airplanes carry people to visit friends and family far away, and they make it easier to see new places. They also carry mail, food, and many other materials that we use every day.

medical helicopter

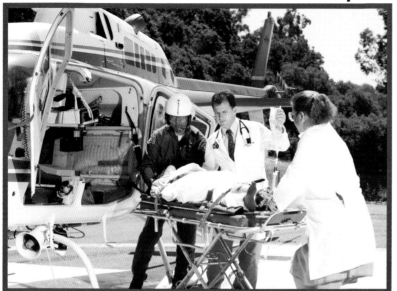

TWIDDLEBUG TRIVIA

Helicopters can't fly as high as planes, but they can rise straight up in the air.

Helicopters can also stay in place in the air—this is called hovering.

Special planes and helicopters can get to places that regular planes cannot, to find and rescue people who need help. Helicopters can take people who are sick or hurt to a hospital faster than an ambulance, because they don't need to travel on roads and can land right on the roof of a hospital.

And did you know that helicopters can even fly backward?

Planes and helicopters can deliver important supplies to places where they are needed. They can also help to put out forest fires by carrying water to drop on a fire from above.

Flying machines are full of surprises!

Some pilots like to fly their planes in loops and twirls. **Stunt planes** are built especially to do these amazing tricks.

Oh my! We have seen so many machines that fly. But there are even more! Look!

Seaplanes have long pontoons instead of wheels, so that they can land on water.

Gliders are planes that don't need an engine to fly. Another plane tows them into the air. Once they're up there, they can keep flying on their own.

Can you see what's missing on this plane? It has no wings! Instead, the body of the plane creates enough lift for it to fly without wings.

This plane is called a **flying wing**. Can you guess why?

Many people work together to make planes fly and rockets blast off.

Pilots are the people who drive planes. Just like in a car, they use tools such as a steering wheel to control the plane. People on the ground called **air traffic controllers** keep track of the planes and talk with the pilots to help them do their job.

Mission Control

Flight mechanics keep planes in good working order and safe to fly.

Lots of people on the ground work hard to make planes and rockets take off, fly, and land safely.

pilot

flight attendant

Flight attendants help passengers stay safe and comfortable.